One More Frog

On **Monday**,

Nick looked at the six fat tadpoles

in the tank.

They were getting much bigger.

Now, all of them had back legs

and front legs as well.

A few of them had tails,

but some had no tails at all.

On **Tuesday**,

Nick shouted, "Mum! Look!

One of my tadpoles

has turned into a little green frog!

I have one frog and five tadpoles."

$$1 + 5 = 6$$

One Frog

On **Thursday**,

one more tadpole

had turned into a frog.

"Now I have two frogs

and four tadpoles," said Nick.

$$2 + 4 = 6$$

One More Frog

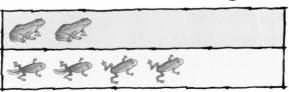

On **Saturday,**

Nick looked in the tank.

One more tadpole

had turned into a frog.

Nick saw three little frogs

and three very fat tadpoles.

$$3 + 3 = 6$$

One More Frog

On **Monday,**

Nick and Dad counted the frogs

and the tadpoles.

"Now you have four frogs

and two tadpoles," said Dad.

$$4 + 2 = 6$$

One More Frog

On **Wednesday**,

Nick looked in the tank.

He saw four frogs and one tadpole.

Where was the other tadpole?

Then Nick saw it sitting on a stone.

It had turned into a frog, too.

Now Nick had five frogs

and one tadpole.

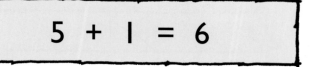

$$5 + 1 = 6$$

One More Frog

On **Friday**,

the last fat tadpole

had turned into a little green frog.

Nick said to Mum,

"All of my tadpoles are frogs now.

So we can take them back

to their home in the big pond."

$$6 + 0 = 6$$

One More Frog

1 + 5 = 6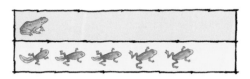

2 + 4 = 6

3 + 3 = 6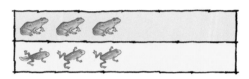

4 + 2 = 6

5 + 1 = 6

6 + 0 = 6